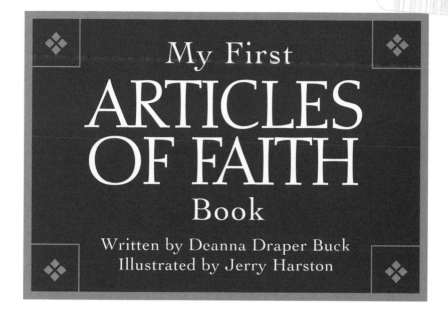

My First
ARTICLES OF FAITH
Book

Written by Deanna Draper Buck
Illustrated by Jerry Harston

Weston Poffenberger

This book belongs to:

Mom

Presented by:

2014

Date:

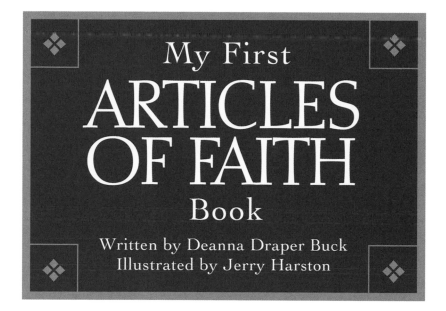

My First
ARTICLES OF FAITH
Book

Written by Deanna Draper Buck
Illustrated by Jerry Harston

DESERET
BOOK

SALT LAKE CITY, UTAH

Text © 2000 Deanna Draper Buck
Illustrations © 2000 Jerry Harston
Illustration of Thomas S. Monson © 2011 Casey Nelson

DESERET BOOK is a registered trademark of Deseret Book Company.

Visit us at DeseretBook.com

First printing in board book format 2000
First printing in paperbound 2008

ISBN 1-57345-839-2 (board book)
ISBN 978-1-59038-931-7 (paperbound)

Printed in Reynosa, Mexico 03/13
R. R. Donnelley, Reynosa, Mexico

10   9   8   7   6   5   4

To my parents,
Rulon and Donna Widdison Draper,
who taught me the gospel

After The Church of Jesus Christ of Latter-day Saints was organized, people wanted to know what "Mormons" believed. The Prophet Joseph Smith wrote a letter to John Wentworth, a newspaper editor, explaining our beliefs. Part of that letter became known as the Articles of Faith.

Joseph Smith wrote that we believe in God and in Jesus Christ and in the Holy Ghost.

1. We believe in God, the Eternal Father, and in His Son, Jesus Christ, and in the Holy Ghost.

The Godhead

Together, Heavenly Father, Jesus, and the Holy Ghost are the Godhead. Heavenly Father is the father of our spirits, and He and Jesus have perfect bodies of flesh and bones. Jesus is Heavenly Father's Only Begotten Son. Jesus created the world and is our Savior. The Holy Ghost is a spirit and doesn't have a physical body. He whispers to us in a still small voice and helps us to know the difference between right and wrong.

Reverence

If we love Heavenly Father and Jesus, we will want to show reverence for Them. Reverence is a feeling of love and respect. We are showing reverence when we sit quietly and listen in church and when we whisper instead of talk out loud in the chapel. We are being reverent when we walk instead of run in the halls of the church. When we fold our arms, close our eyes, and bow our heads during prayers, we are being reverent.

Prayer

Heavenly Father loves each of us, and He wants us to talk with Him. We talk with Him when we pray. We begin a prayer by saying, "Heavenly Father." Then we thank Him for our parents, our brothers and sisters, our teachers, our friends, our food and clothes, and everything He gives us. Then, if there is something we need, we can ask Him for a blessing. When we finish our prayer, we say, "In the name of Jesus Christ, amen."

 Joseph Smith wrote that we can each choose for ourselves whether or not we will be good and do what Heavenly Father teaches us to do.

2. We believe that men will be punished for their own sins, and not for Adam's transgression.

I Am a Child of God

Before we were born, we were spirits and lived with our Heavenly Father. Jesus was our oldest brother, and we were all brothers and sisters. When it was time, each of us came to earth and was born. We came to earth to get a body and to learn to choose the right. Heavenly Father and Jesus love us, and They want us to be happy. If we keep the commandments, we can go back and live with Them again in heaven.

Joseph Smith wrote that Jesus is our Savior.

3. We believe that through the Atonement of Christ, all mankind may be saved, by obedience to the laws and ordinances of the Gospel.

The Gospel and the Atonement

Jesus is our Savior. Because of Him, we will be resurrected (come alive again) after we die. Because of Him, we can also be forgiven when we do something wrong, if we say we are sorry and promise to do better. The word *gospel* means "good news." The good news is that because of Jesus we can live forever with Heavenly Father and with our families.

The Sacrament

The most important reason we go to church on Sundays is not to go to Primary or Sunday School, but to take the sacrament. When we take the sacrament, we should think about Jesus and how much He loves each of us. The bread reminds us of Jesus' body and the water helps us remember His blood and how He suffered and died for us. When we take the sacrament, we should think about when we were baptized and the promise we made to remember Jesus and to keep His commandments. If we remember Him and keep His commandments, He promises to send His Spirit to be with us.

Joseph Smith explained the first principles and ordinances of the gospel to John Wentworth.

4. We believe that the first principles and ordinances of the Gospel are: first, Faith in the Lord Jesus Christ; second, Repentance; third, Baptism by immersion for the remission of sins; fourth, Laying on of hands for the gift of the Holy Ghost.

Faith

We can't see Heavenly Father or Jesus, but we can know that They are real and that They love us. Having faith is believing in something that is true that we can't see. When we are sick, we can have faith that we will get better. When we are sad or frightened, we can have faith that the Holy Ghost will comfort us. Most important, we can have faith that, because of Jesus, after we die we will be resurrected and can live with Heavenly Father and Jesus in heaven. Having faith helps us to be happy.

Repentance

Heavenly Father and Jesus know that it is hard for us to always remember to do what is right. When we do something wrong, we feel sad until we are forgiven. We can be forgiven if we repent. To repent, we say we are sorry and promise to try harder to keep the commandments. When we truly repent, Jesus forgives us, and we feel clean and happy again.

Baptism

When we are eight years old, we are old enough to know the difference between right and wrong. We can then be baptized. When we are baptized, we promise to follow Jesus and keep His commandments, and He promises to forgive us for the things we do wrong. Being baptized is the first step in becoming a member of Christ's Church. The day you are baptized is one of the most important days of your life.

The Gift of the Holy Ghost

After we are baptized, we are confirmed a member of the Church and are given the gift of the Holy Ghost. The Holy Ghost helps us know right from wrong. He helps us remember important things. The Holy Ghost also comforts us when we are sad or frightened. The gift of the Holy Ghost is a gift from Heavenly Father and Jesus that will help us our whole life.

 Joseph Smith explained that men must have authority from God to do His work here on earth. That authority is called the priesthood.

5. We believe that a man must be called of God, by prophecy, and by the laying on of hands by those who are in authority, to preach the Gospel and administer in the ordinances thereof.

Priesthood

The priesthood is a special power from Heavenly Father that allows men to serve others in the name of God. Boys can hold the Aaronic Priesthood after they turn twelve years old. Grown-up men can hold the Melchizedek Priesthood and can go on missions, give the gift of the Holy Ghost, or give blessings to sick people.

Joseph Smith explained to John Wentworth that The Church of Jesus Christ of Latter-day Saints is the "restored" Church of Christ and has the same officers as the church Jesus organized when He was living on the earth.

6. We believe in the same organization that existed in the Primitive Church, namely, apostles, prophets, pastors, teachers, evangelists, and so forth.

Prophets and Apostles

Some prophets and apostles lived long ago, but there are also prophets and apostles living today. They are special men who lead the Church and teach us about Heavenly Father and Jesus. Our prophet is the president of the Church, and he listens to the Lord and receives messages from Him. The prophet then teaches us what Heavenly Father and Jesus want us to do. When we follow the prophet's teachings, we are blessed.

Joseph Smith explained that Heavenly Father gives us blessings called "gifts of the Spirit."

7. We believe in the gift of tongues, prophecy, revelation, visions, healing, interpretation of tongues, and so forth.

The Gifts of the Spirit

One of the gifts of the Spirit is to be able to be healed. When we are sick, we can be healed by the power of the priesthood. Another gift of the Spirit is when a missionary is sent to a foreign land and is able to quickly learn and understand a new language. We are blessed to have a prophet who has the gift of revelation from Heavenly Father. There are many other gifts of the Spirit.

 Joseph Smith told John Wentworth that we believe in and follow the teachings found in the Bible and in the Book of Mormon.

8. We believe the Bible to be the word of God as far as it is translated correctly; we also believe the Book of Mormon to be the word of God.

The Scriptures

The Lord speaks to His prophets, and the prophets write down His words. In our Church we have four sacred books, called scriptures. These four books are the Bible, the Book of Mormon, the Doctrine and Covenants, and the Pearl of Great Price. We read the scriptures to learn the gospel and to find out what Heavenly Father wants us to do. The scriptures are very precious, special books.

Joseph Smith explained that we have a living prophet who receives revelation from God. The Lord guides His Church through the prophet.

9. We believe all that God has revealed, all that He does now reveal, and we believe that He will yet reveal many great and important things pertaining to the Kingdom of God.

Tithing

One of the revelations Joseph Smith received was the law of tithing. Everything we have comes from God. He has asked us to show our thanks by giving back some of what He gives to us. We do this by paying tithing. Tithing is ten percent of what you earn. If you earn ten cents, your tithing is one penny; if you earn one dollar, your tithing is ten cents. We give our tithing to our bishop. The money is used to build temples and chapels and to do the Lord's work. When we pay our tithing, we receive blessings and help the Church grow.

The Word of Wisdom

Joseph Smith also received a revelation called the Word of Wisdom. Heavenly Father made our wonderful bodies and wants us to take good care of them. The Word of Wisdom teaches us not to smoke or use tobacco. It tells us we should not drink alcohol, coffee, or tea. And it explains that we need to eat healthy foods, get enough sleep, and exercise our bodies. When we do these things we will be healthier and happier.

Temples

Another revelation given to Joseph Smith was to build temples. Temples are very special buildings. They are beautiful and also sacred. When you are twelve years old, you can go to the temple and be baptized for the dead. When you are old enough, you can also go to the temple to be married. When we are married in the temple, we can be together with our family members forever. There are temples being built all over the world. Each of them is the House of the Lord.

Joseph Smith said in his letter to John Wentworth that Jesus would return to the earth, just as He had promised the people in the Bible and in the Book of Mormon.

10. We believe in the literal gathering of Israel and in the restoration of the Ten Tribes; that Zion (the New Jerusalem) will be built upon the American continent; that Christ will reign personally upon the earth; and, that the earth will be renewed and receive its paradisiacal glory.

Missionary Work

Before Jesus returns to reign on earth, the gospel must be taught in every land. Heavenly Father and Jesus love everyone and They want *all* of their children to know about The Church of Jesus Christ of Latter-day Saints. Missionaries are sent all over the world to teach the "good news" that the gospel has been restored. You can be a missionary by inviting your friends to come to church with you and by being a good example. When you are old enough, you can go on a full-time mission and teach the gospel.

The Second Coming

After Jesus was resurrected, He visited for a time with the people in Jerusalem and also with the Nephites. He promised that after He went to live in heaven, He would return one day to earth. When Jesus comes again, He will be our King, and everyone will know who He is and want to follow His teachings. There will be peace on earth for a thousand years. That time will be called the Millennium.

Our Beautiful World

Jesus made this beautiful world. He filled it with oceans, rivers, mountains, forests, flowers, clouds, and good things to eat. Jesus wants us to take good care of the earth. We can all help keep it beautiful by throwing papers and cans in the trash instead of on the ground. We can help by planting trees and flowers and gardens. When we do these things, we show Jesus that we are thankful for our beautiful world. When He comes again, the world will be made even more beautiful, like it was in the Garden of Eden.

 Joseph Smith wrote that everyone should be free to worship God in the way he or she feels is right.

11. We claim the privilege of worshiping Almighty God according to the dictates of our own conscience, and allow all men the same privilege, let them worship how, where, or what they may.

Loving Others and Being Kind

In many ways all of us are the same, and in many ways, each of us is different. But we are all children of Heavenly Father, and He loves us and wants us to love each other. Jesus taught that we should treat other people the way we would like to be treated.

Even though some people look, walk, talk, or do things differently from the way we do, we should still be kind to them and be their friend.

Joseph Smith told John Wentworth that Latter-day Saints believe in obeying the law and in being good citizens of the countries where they live.

12. We believe in being subject to kings, presidents, rulers, and magistrates, in obeying, honoring, and sustaining the law.

Obeying the Law

When we play a game, we need to follow the rules, so that everyone knows what to do, has a fair chance, and gets to take a turn. We also need to obey the laws of the country where we live. When we obey the law, it makes everyone happier and keeps us all safe.

Choosing the Right

Even when we are young, we can tell the difference between right and wrong. We feel happy when we do good things, and we feel mean and sad when we don't. We feel happy when we share, obey our parents, tell the truth, and help other people. We feel sad when we disobey, tell a lie, or fight or quarrel. Heavenly Father wants us to obey His commandments because He knows that when we do, we are happier.

 The last Article of Faith explains that every good thing in the world is part of the gospel of Jesus Christ. As members of His Church, we should do everything we can to be better people.

13. We believe in being honest, true, chaste, benevolent, virtuous, and in doing good to all men; indeed, we may say that we follow the admonition of Paul—We believe all things, we hope all things, we have endured many things, and hope to be able to endure all things. If there is anything virtuous, lovely, or of good report or praiseworthy, we seek after these things.

Honesty

Heavenly Father and Jesus always tell the truth. Because They have promised, we know that if we keep the commandments, They will forgive our sins; we know that we will be resurrected; and we know that we can live with our families and with Heavenly Father and Jesus forever. We are trying to be like Jesus when we tell the truth, when we don't steal or cheat, and when we keep our promises.

Kindness

Heavenly Father and Jesus want us to be kind. When we think about other people's feelings, we will want to be nice to them. If we are kind, we will share with others and help them if they are hurt or sad. We will say nice things and be a friend. If we have a pet, we will take good care of it and not tease or hurt it. Being kind to other people or to animals makes us feel happy.

Service

We can show Heavenly Father and Jesus that we love Them by doing nice things for other people. This is called giving service. We can serve our own family by helping set the table and washing the dishes. We can serve our brothers and sisters and friends by sharing with them. We can serve our mother by picking up our toys and clothes and by playing nicely with our brothers and sisters. We can serve our father by helping him do yard work. When we help others, it makes us feel happy. It makes those we help feel happy, too.

About the Author

Award-winning, bestselling author DEANNA DRAPER BUCK and her husband have been married for over forty years. They currently live in Hooper, Utah, where they enjoy gardening, the Great Salt Lake, and entertaining their nineteen grandchildren. Deanna has written nine LDS children's books, explaining gospel principles, Church history, and scriptures stories in a simplified style.

About the Illustrator

JERRY HARSTON held a degree in graphic design and illustrated more than thirty children's books. He received many honors for his art, and his clients included numerous Fortune 500 corporations. Jerry passed away in December 2009.